The Artwork Of Melissa Hiatt

2010 - 2014

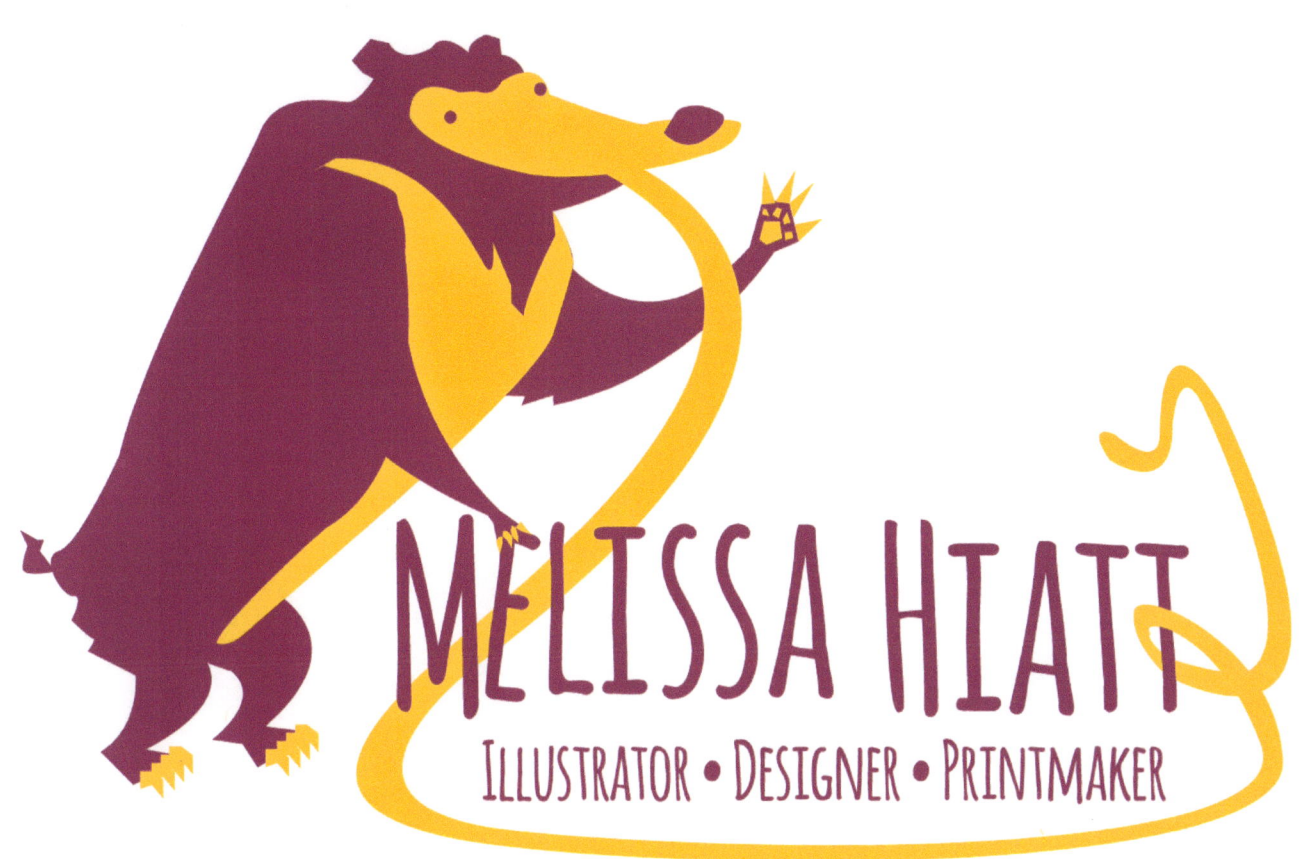

MELISSA HIATT
Illustrator • Designer • Printmaker

Contact Me
614-746-3933
MelissaHiatt.com
MHiattDraws@gmail.com

Follow My Work
Melissahiattillustration.tumblr.com
Facebook.com/MelissaHiattIllustrate

Behance.net/MhiattIllstrator

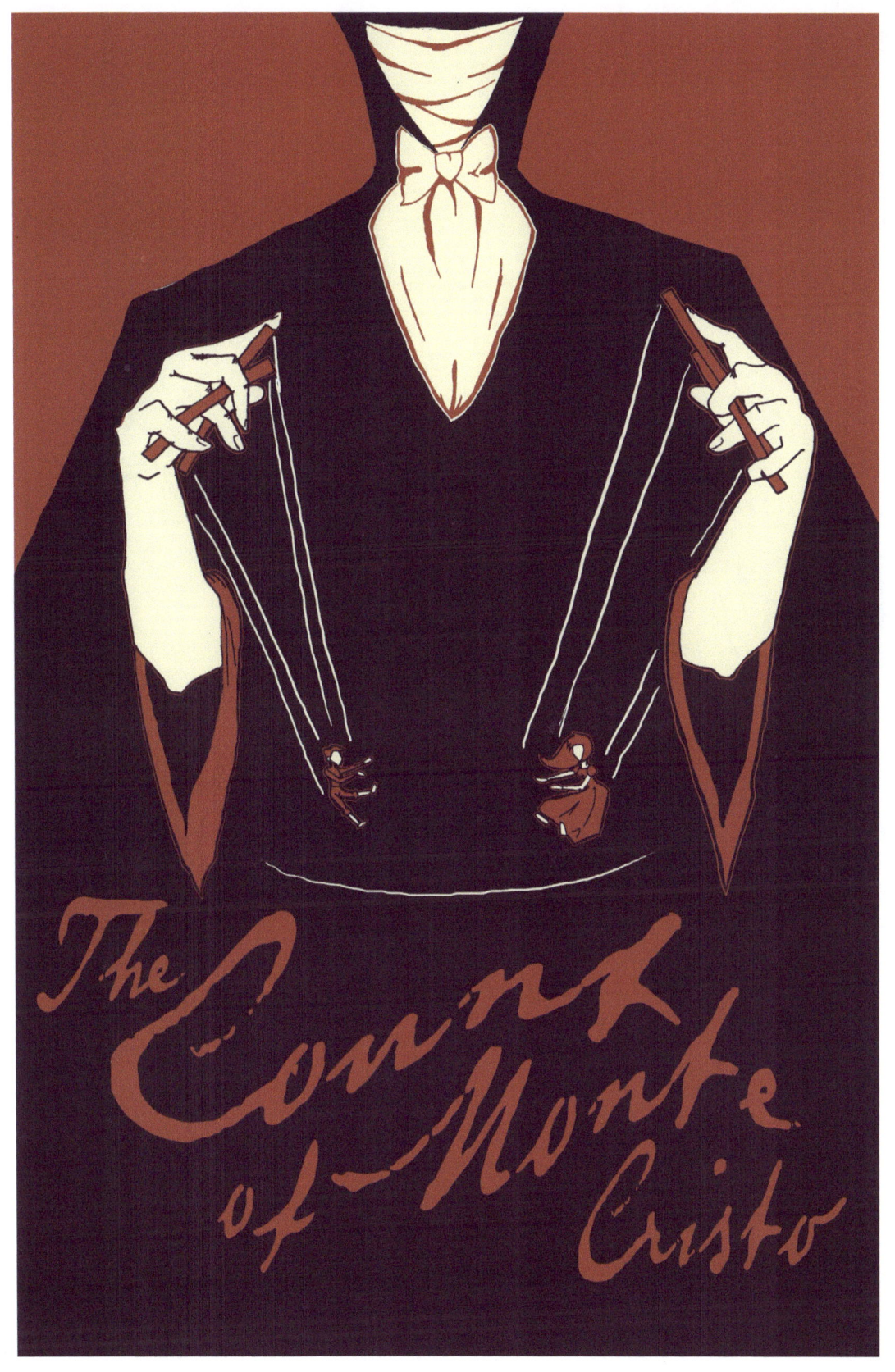

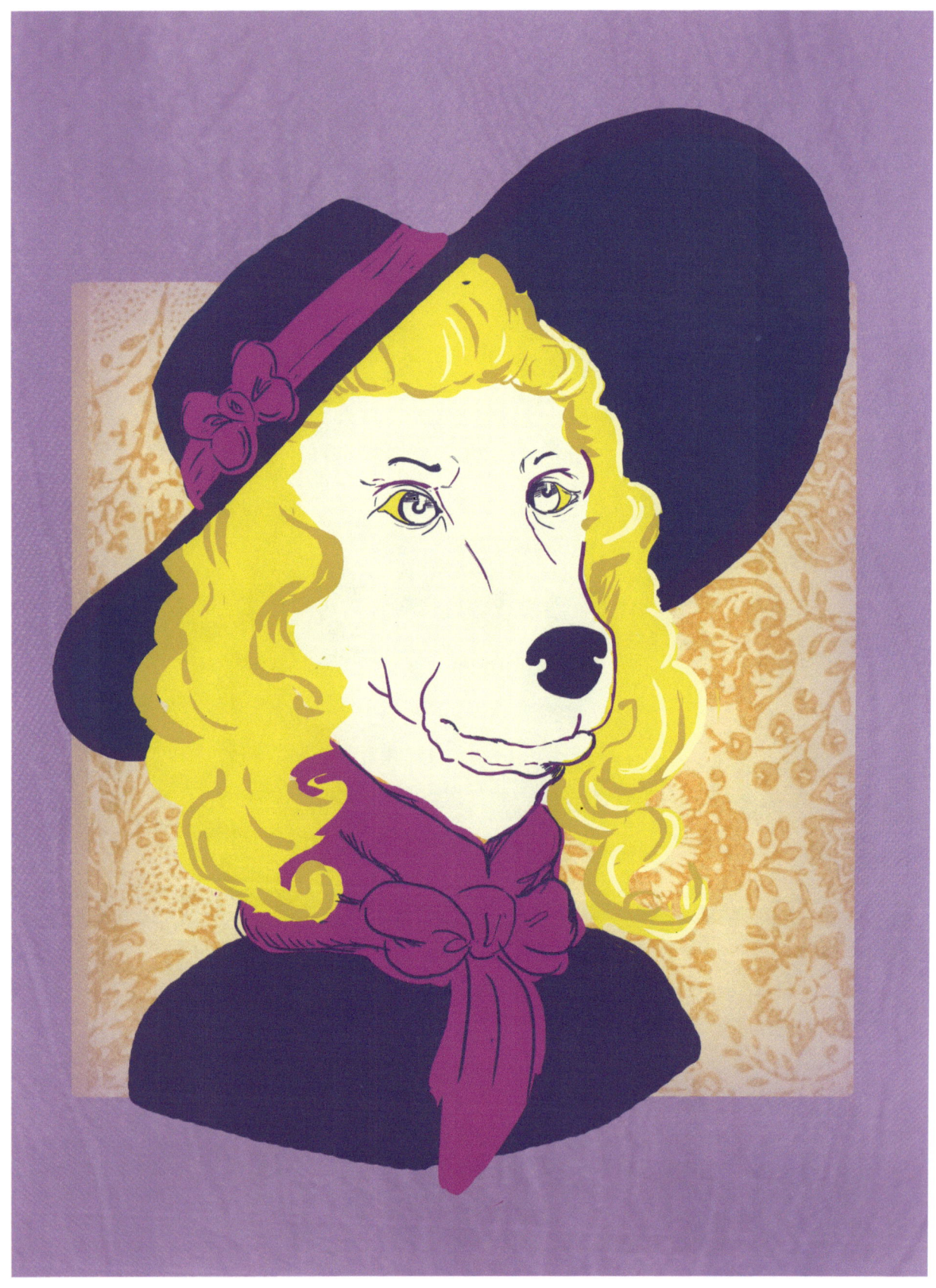

Fancy 2012

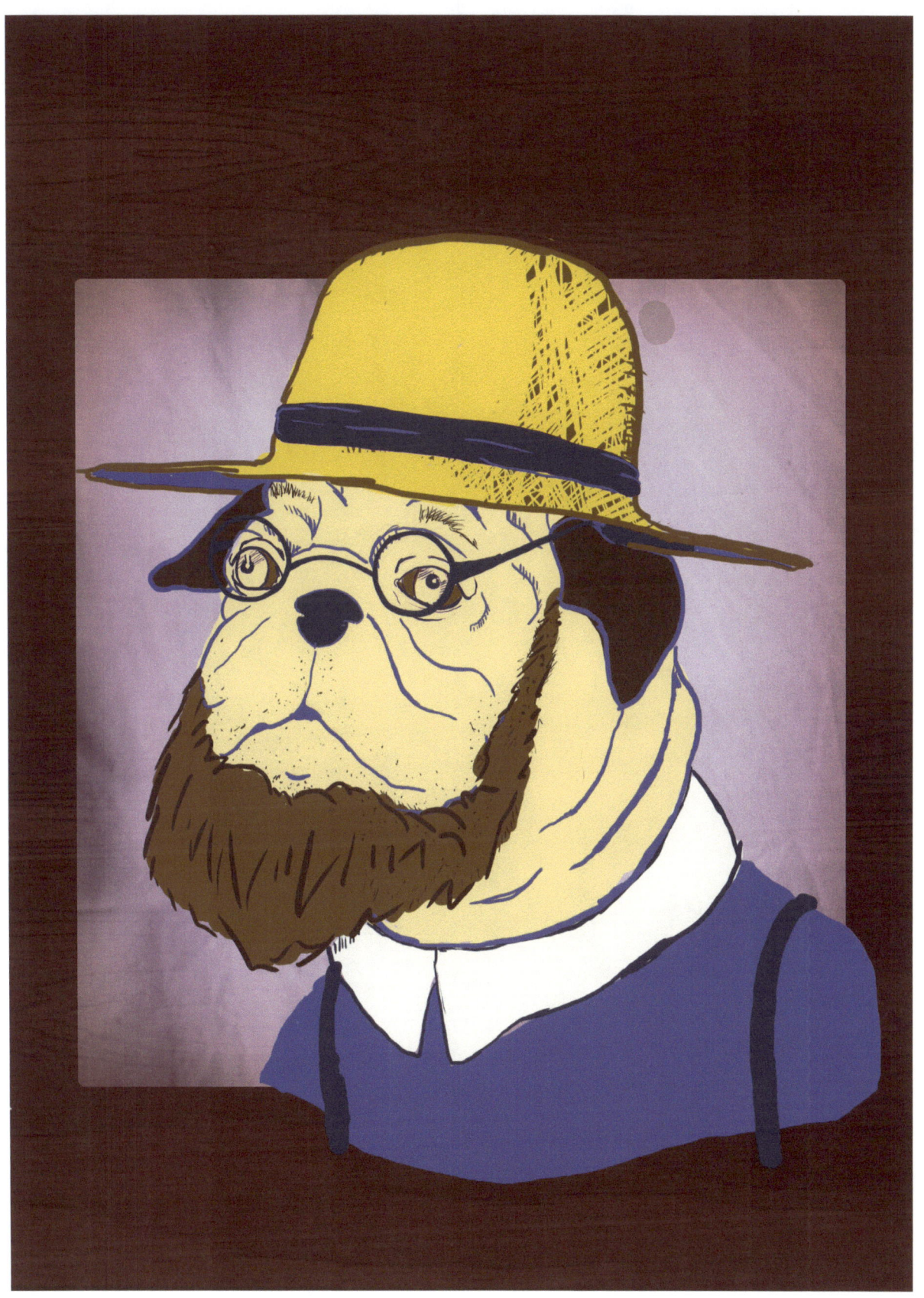

Plain 2012

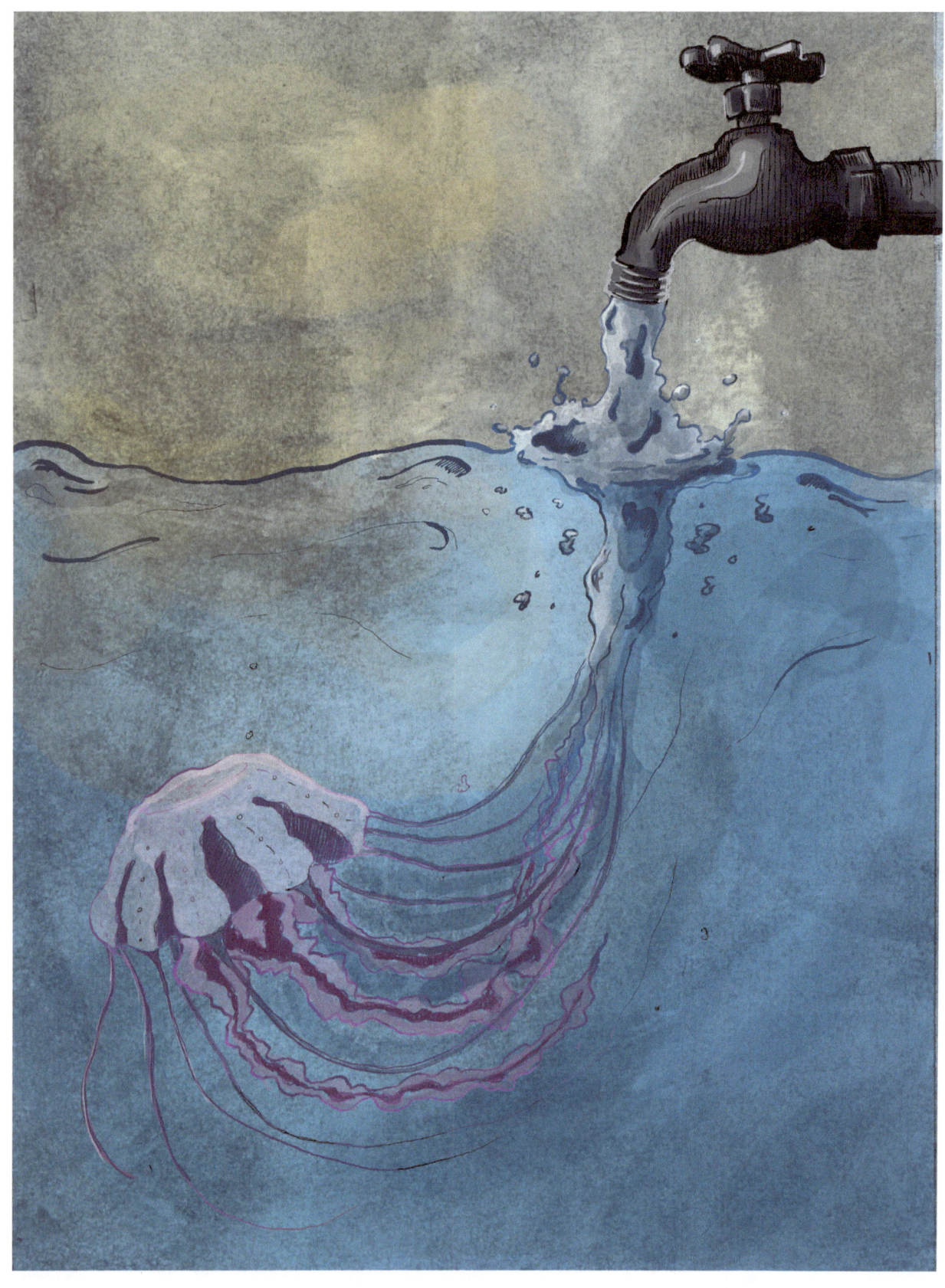

99% Water 2011

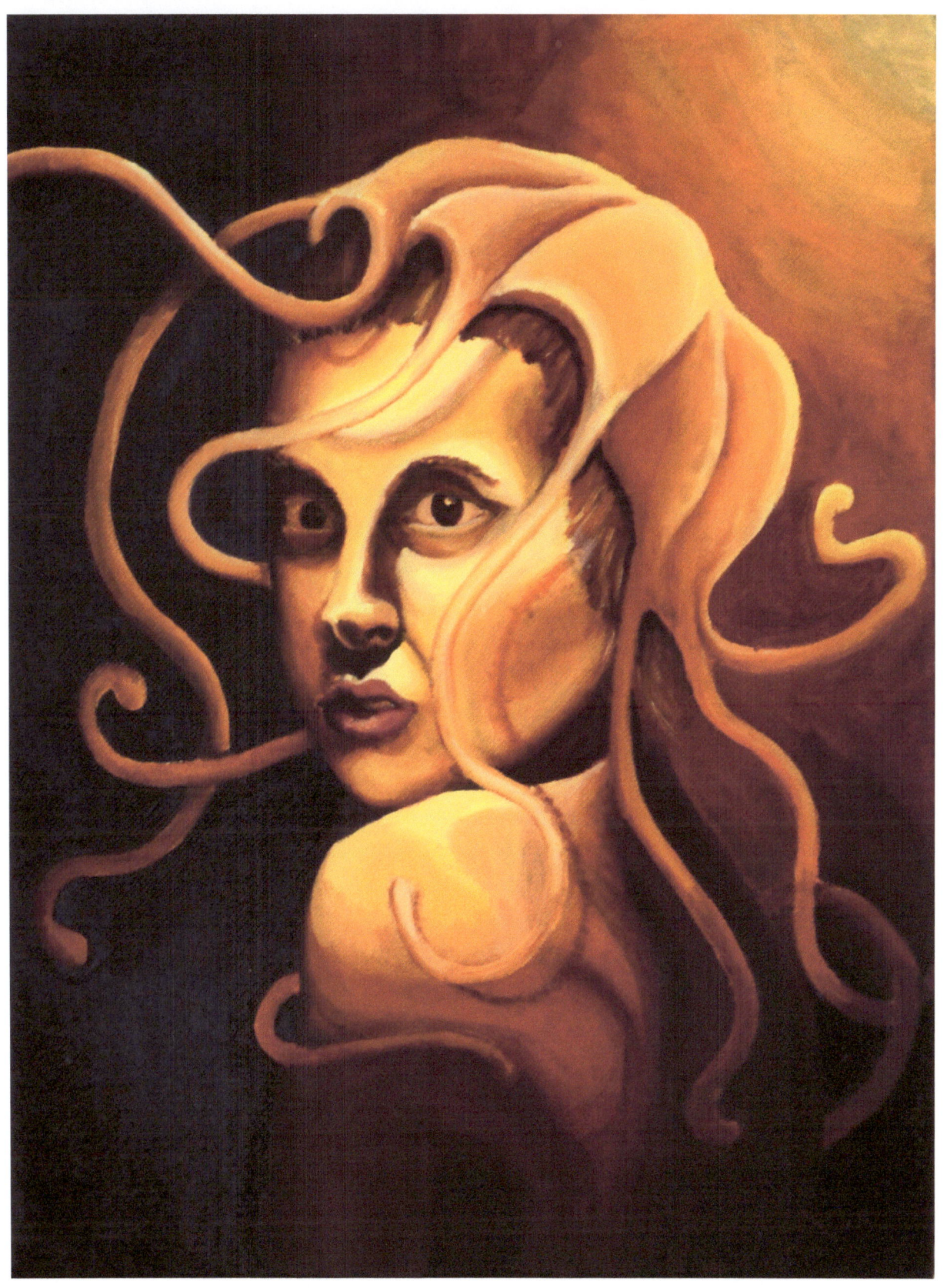

Hats 2011

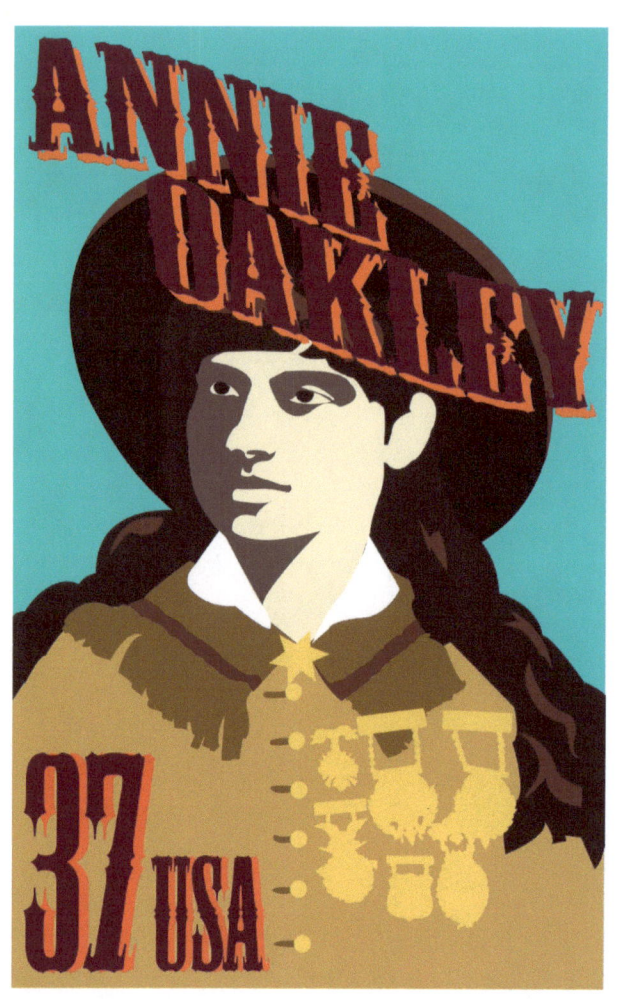

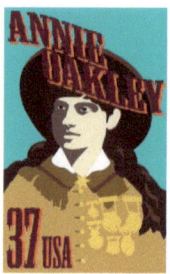

Annie Oakley Stamp 2013

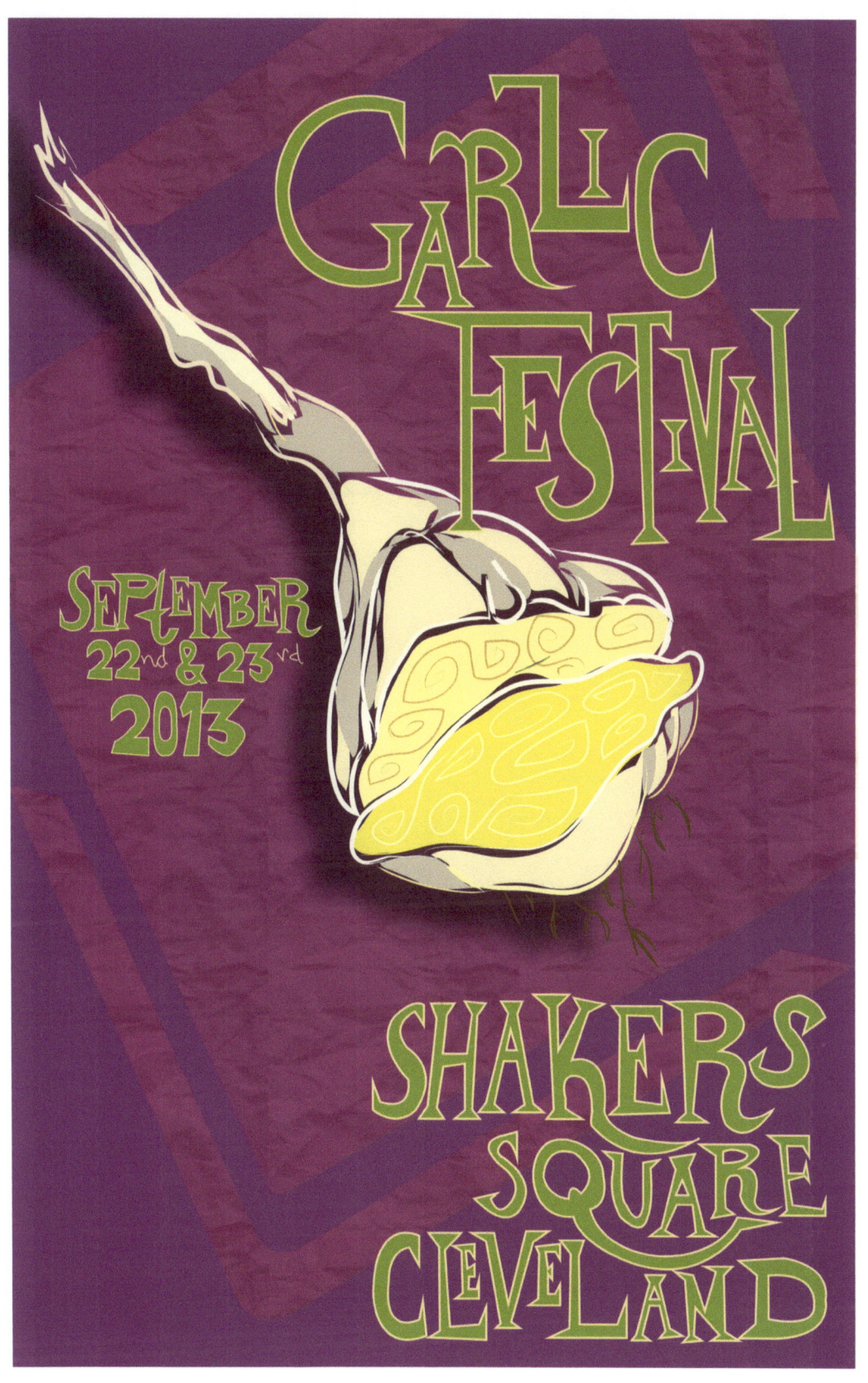

Garlic Festival 2011

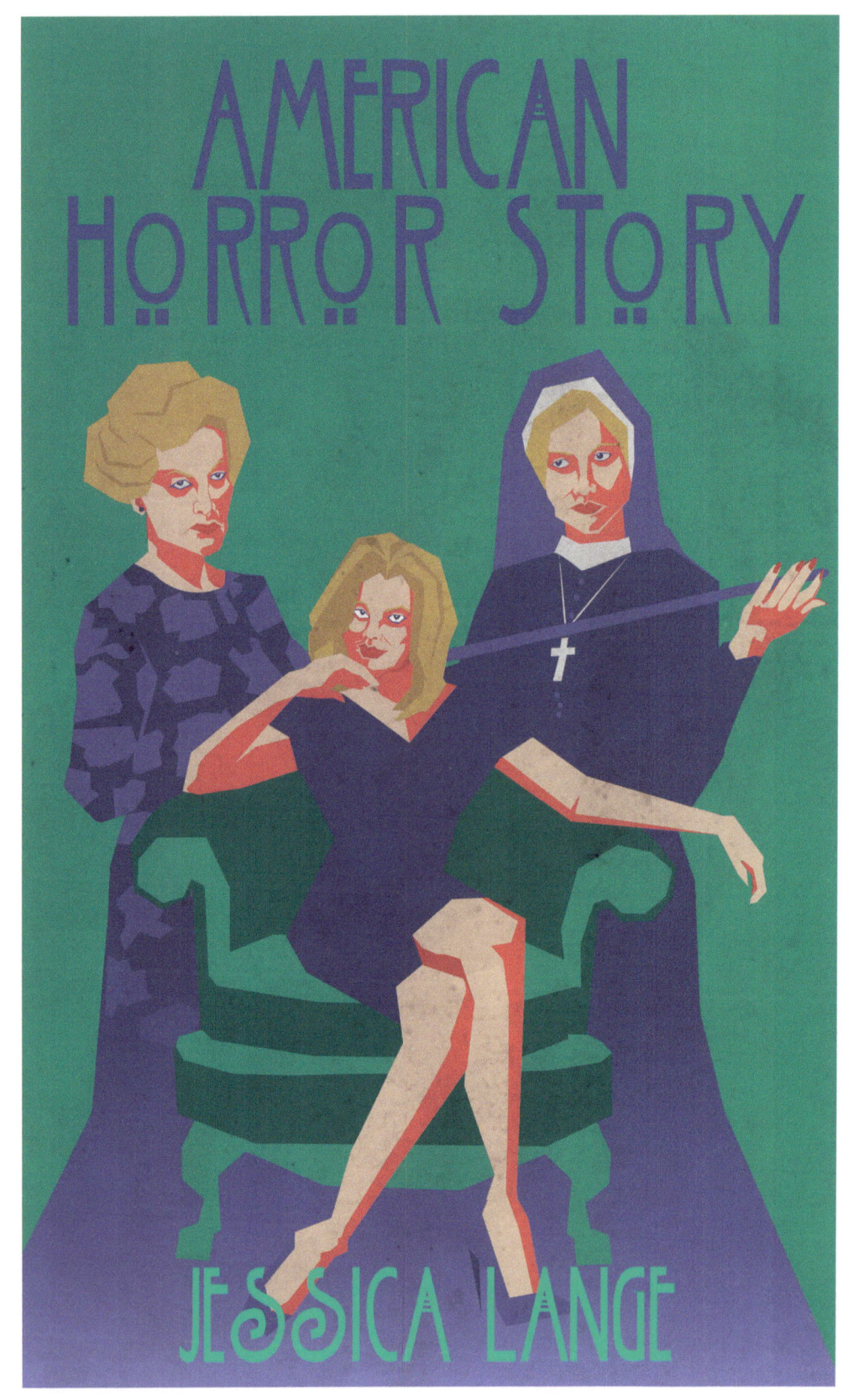

Jessica Lange: American Horror Story Poster 2013

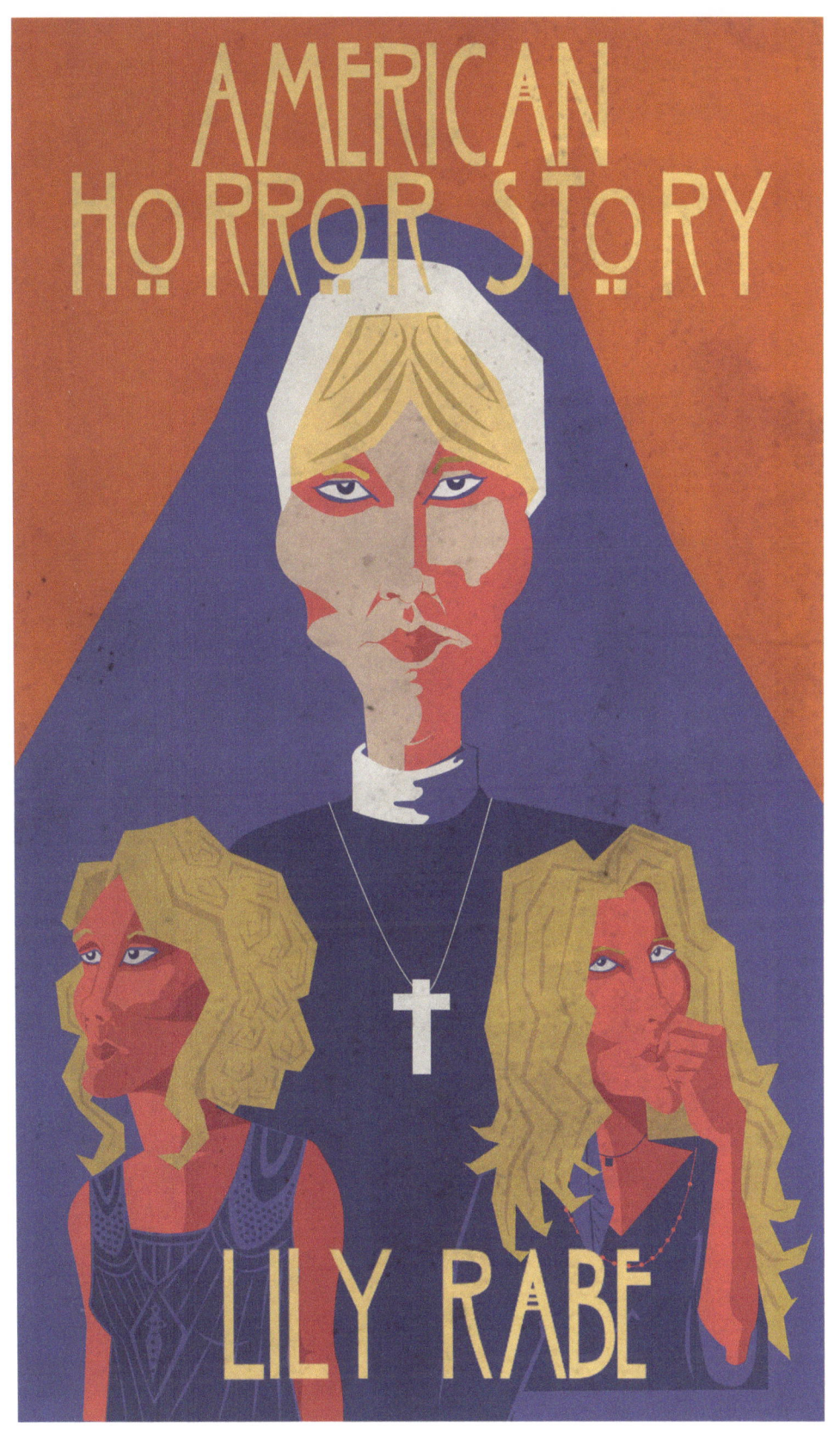

Lily Rabe: American Horror Story Poster 2013

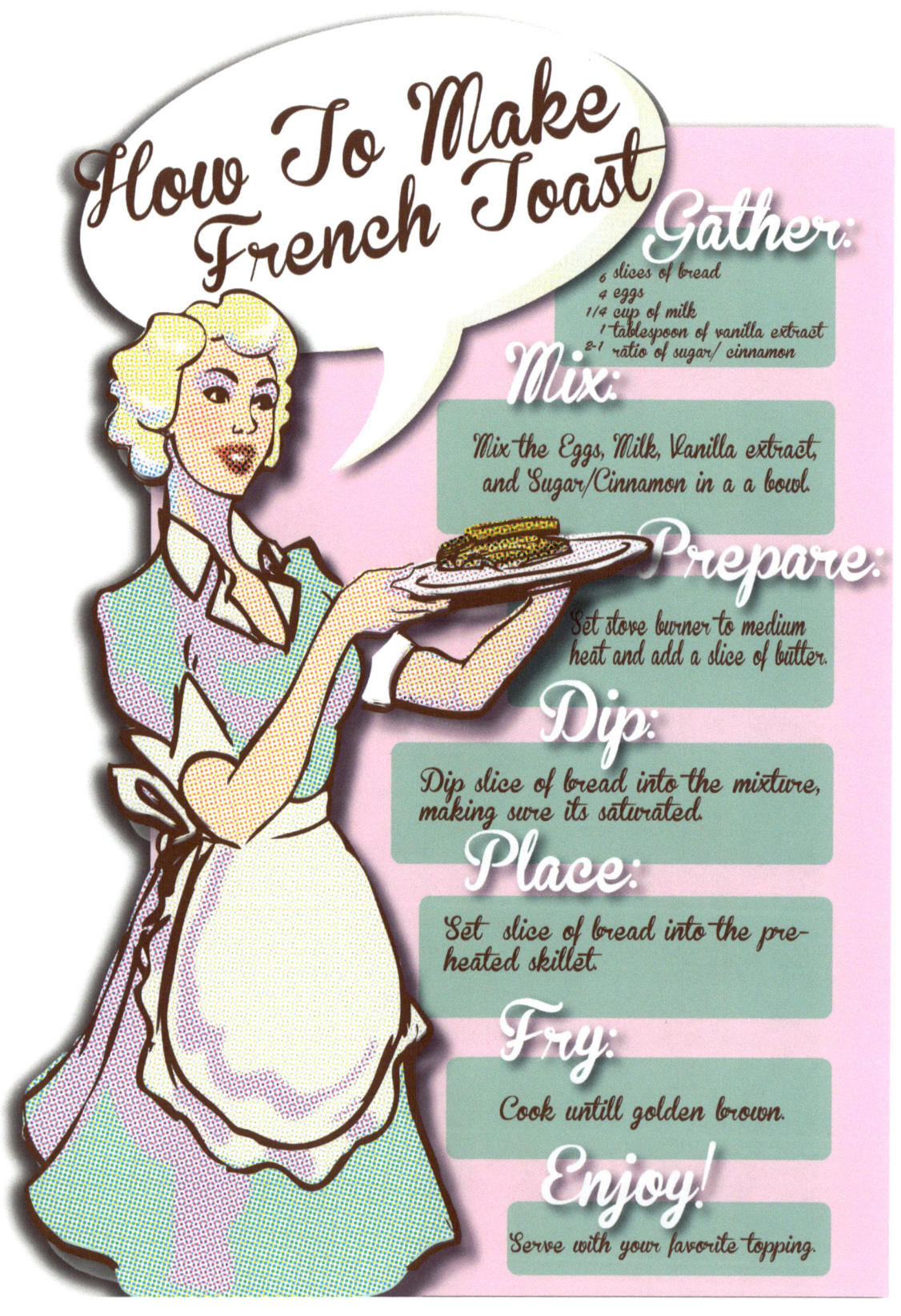

How To Make French Toast

Gather:
6 slices of bread
4 eggs
1/4 cup of milk
1 tablespoon of vanilla extract
2-1 ratio of sugar/ cinnamon

Mix:
Mix the Eggs, Milk, Vanilla extract, and Sugar/Cinnamon in a a bowl.

Prepare:
Set stove burner to medium heat and add a slice of butter.

Dip:
Dip slice of bread into the mixture, making sure its saturated.

Place:
Set slice of bread into the pre-heated skillet.

Fry:
Cook untill golden brown.

Enjoy!
Serve with your favorite topping.

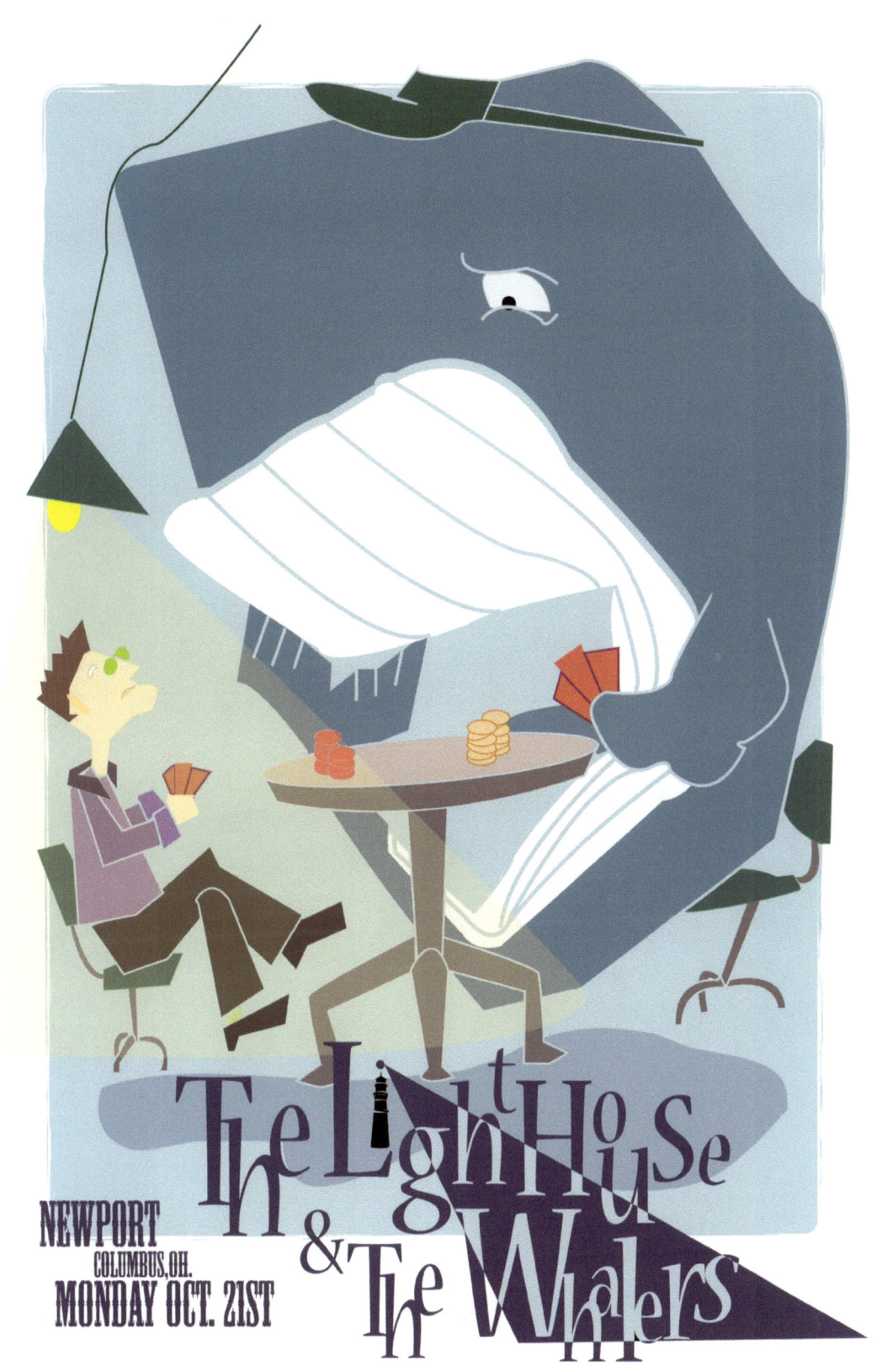

The Lighthouse & The Whalers Gig Poster 2012

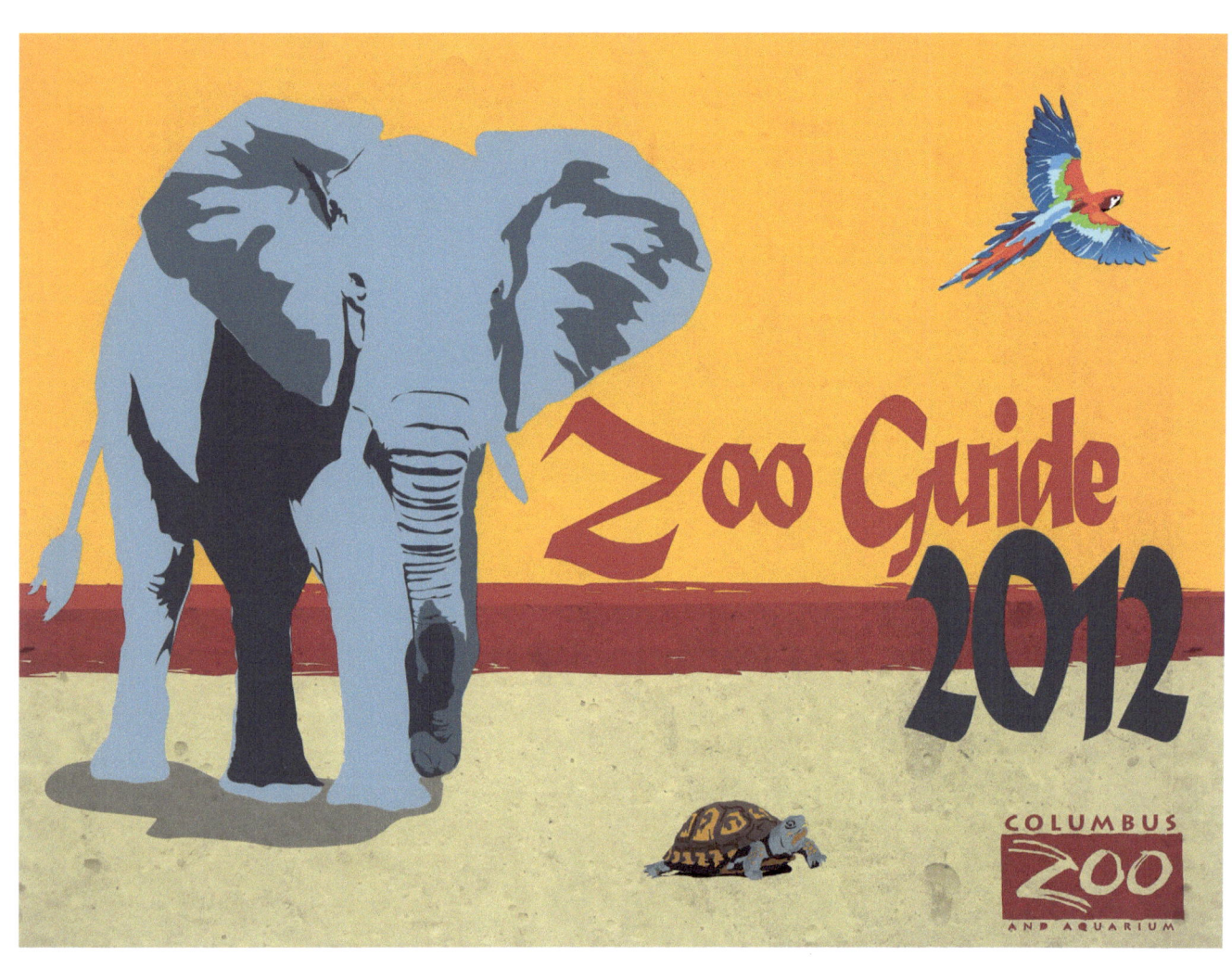

Zoo Brochure : Front 2012

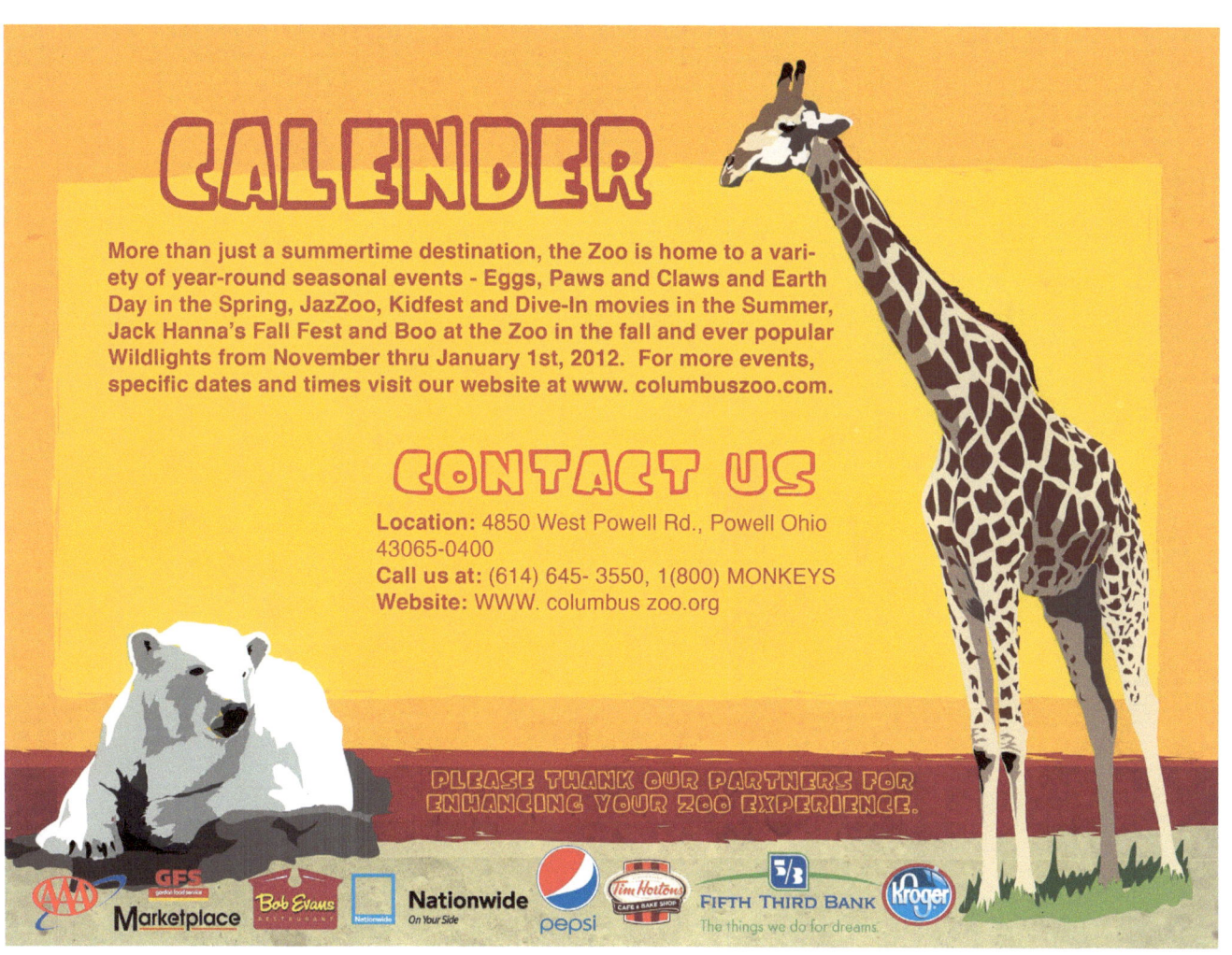

CALENDER

More than just a summertime destination, the Zoo is home to a variety of year-round seasonal events - Eggs, Paws and Claws and Earth Day in the Spring, JazZoo, Kidfest and Dive-In movies in the Summer, Jack Hanna's Fall Fest and Boo at the Zoo in the fall and ever popular Wildlights from November thru January 1st, 2012. For more events, specific dates and times visit our website at www. columbuszoo.com.

CONTACT US

Location: 4850 West Powell Rd., Powell Ohio 43065-0400
Call us at: (614) 645- 3550, 1(800) MONKEYS
Website: WWW. columbus zoo.org

PLEASE THANK OUR PARTNERS FOR ENHANCING YOUR ZOO EXPERIENCE.

Zoo Brochure : Back 2012

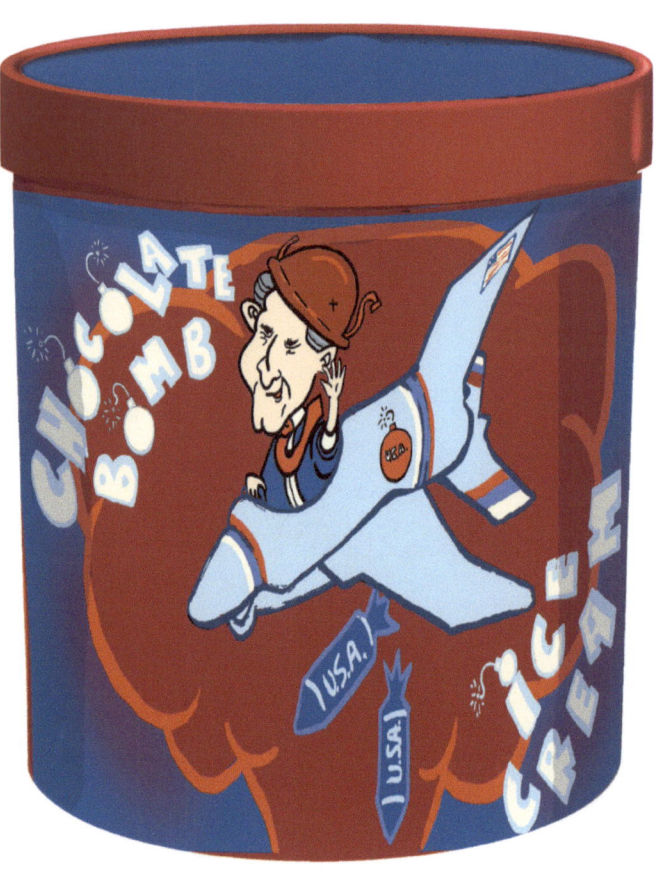

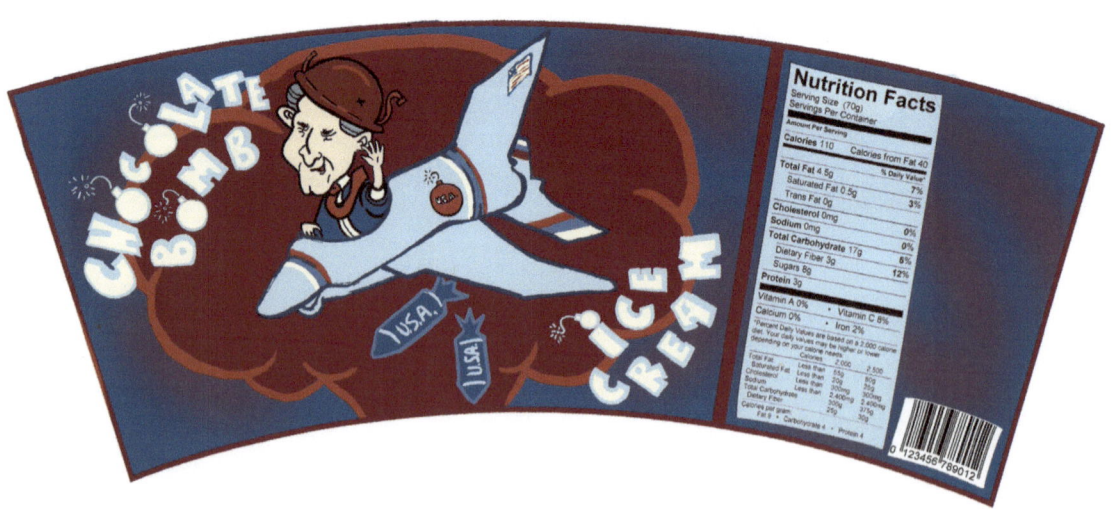

Presidential Ice Cream Label 2013

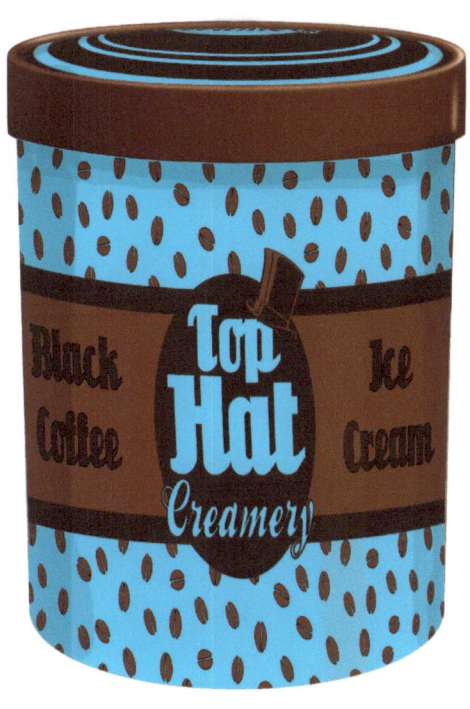

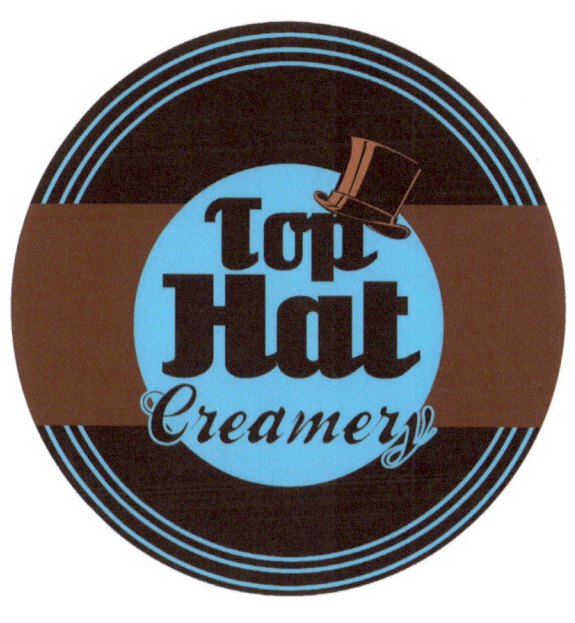

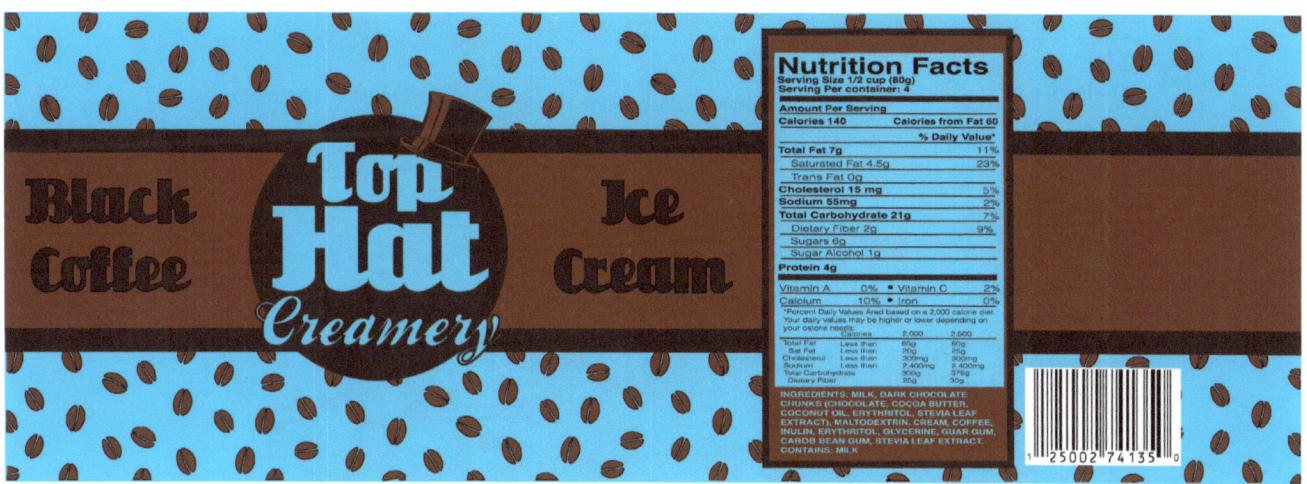

Nutrition Facts
Serving Size 1/2 cup (80g)
Serving Per container: 4

Amount Per Serving

Calories 140   Calories from Fat 60

% Daily Value*

Total Fat 7g   11%
Saturated Fat 4.5g   23%
Trans Fat 0g
Cholesterol 15 mg   5%
Sodium 55mg   2%
Total Carbohydrate 21g 7%
Dietary Fiber 2g   9%
Sugars 6g
Sugar Alcohol 1g

Protein 4g

Vitamin A   0% • Vitamin C   2%
Calcium   10% • Iron   0%

*Percent Daily Values Areil based on a 2,000 calorie diet.
Your daily values may be higher or lower depending on
your calorie needs.

		Calories	2,000	2,600
Total Fat	Less than		65g	80g
Sat Fat	Less than		20g	25g
Cholesterol	Less than		300mg	300mg
Sodium	Less than		2,400mg	2,400mg
Total Carbohydrate			300g	375g
Dietary Fiber			25g	30g

INGREDIENTS: MILK, DARK CHOCOLATE
CHUNKS (CHOCOLATE, COCOA BUTTER,
COCONUT OIL, ERYTHRITOL, STEVIA LEAF
EXTRACT), MALTODEXTRIN, CREAM, COFFEE,
INULIN, ERYTHRITOL, GLYCERINE, GUAR GUM,
CAROB BEAN GUM, STEVIA LEAF EXTRACT.
CONTAINS: MILK

1 25002 74135 0

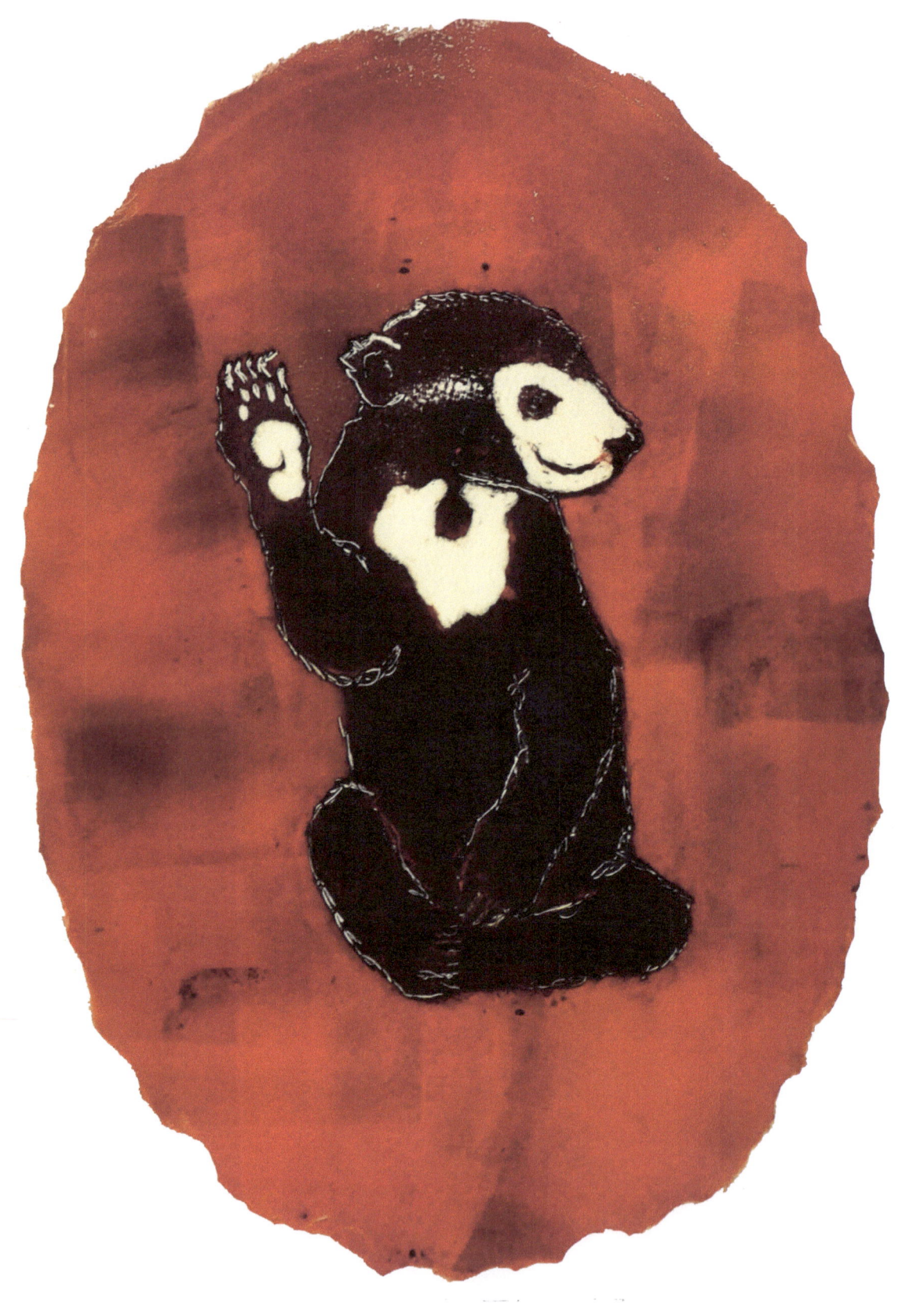

Sun Bear 2014

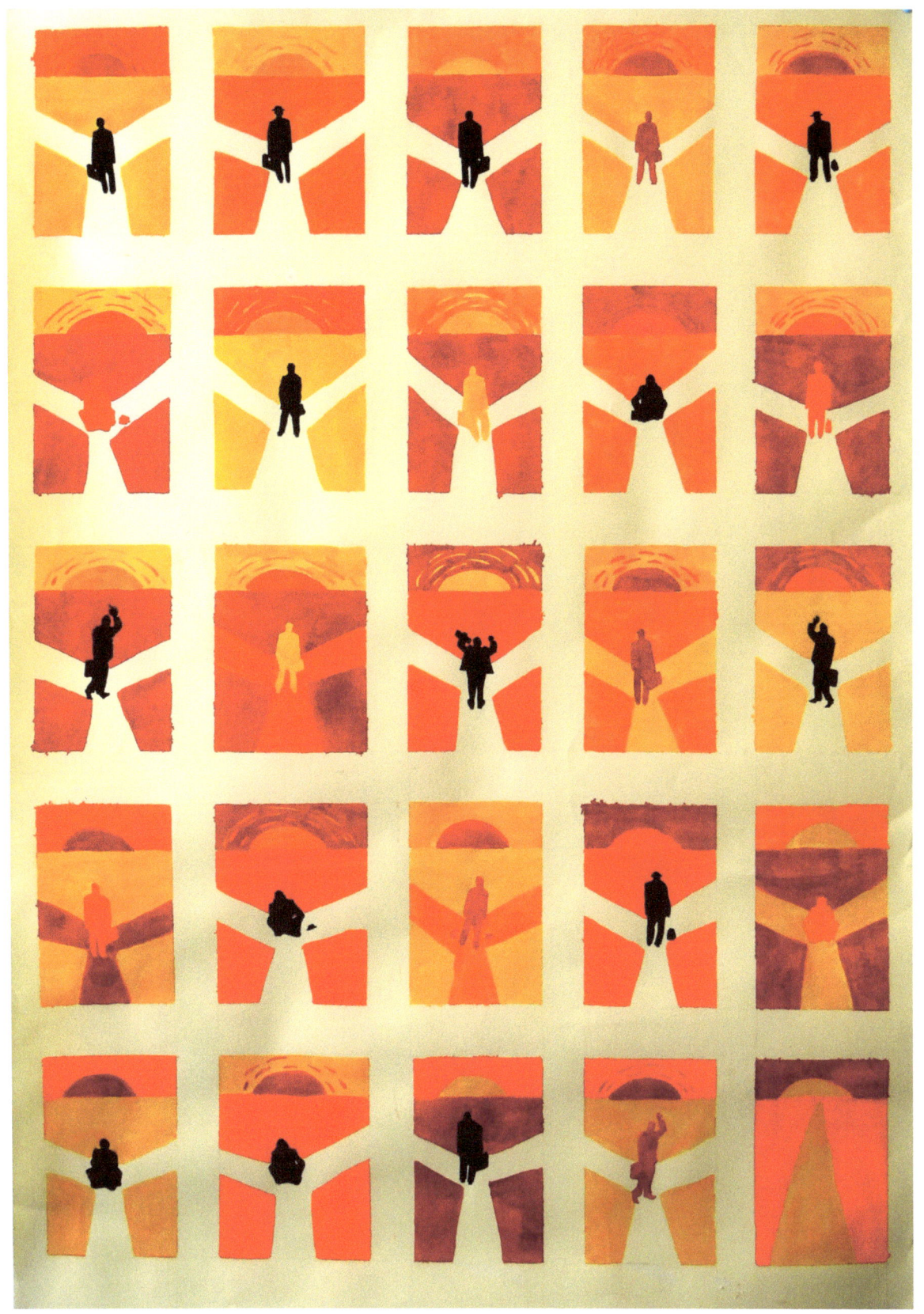

The Road 2013

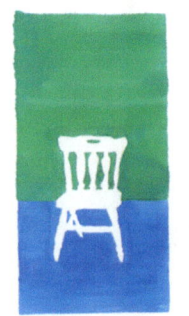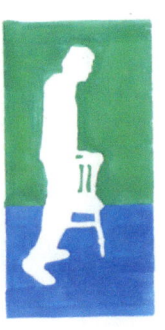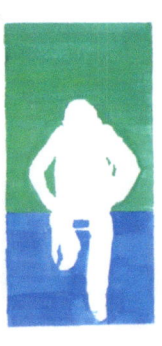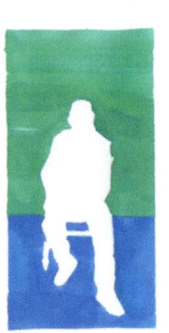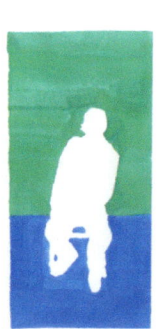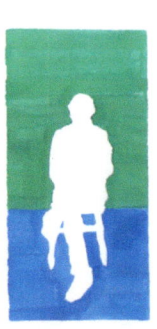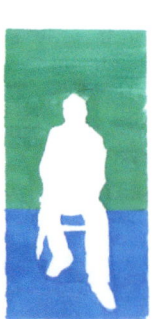

Waiting 2013

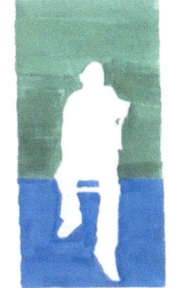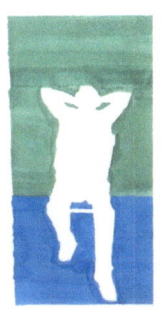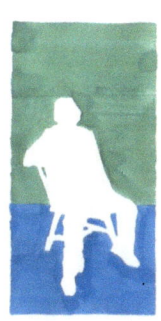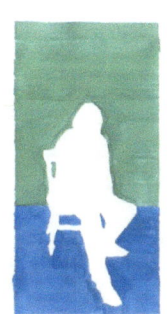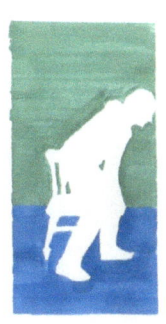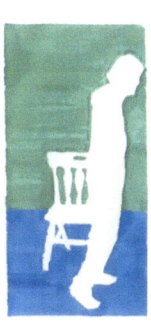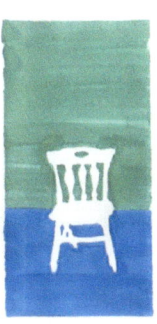

Waiting Continued

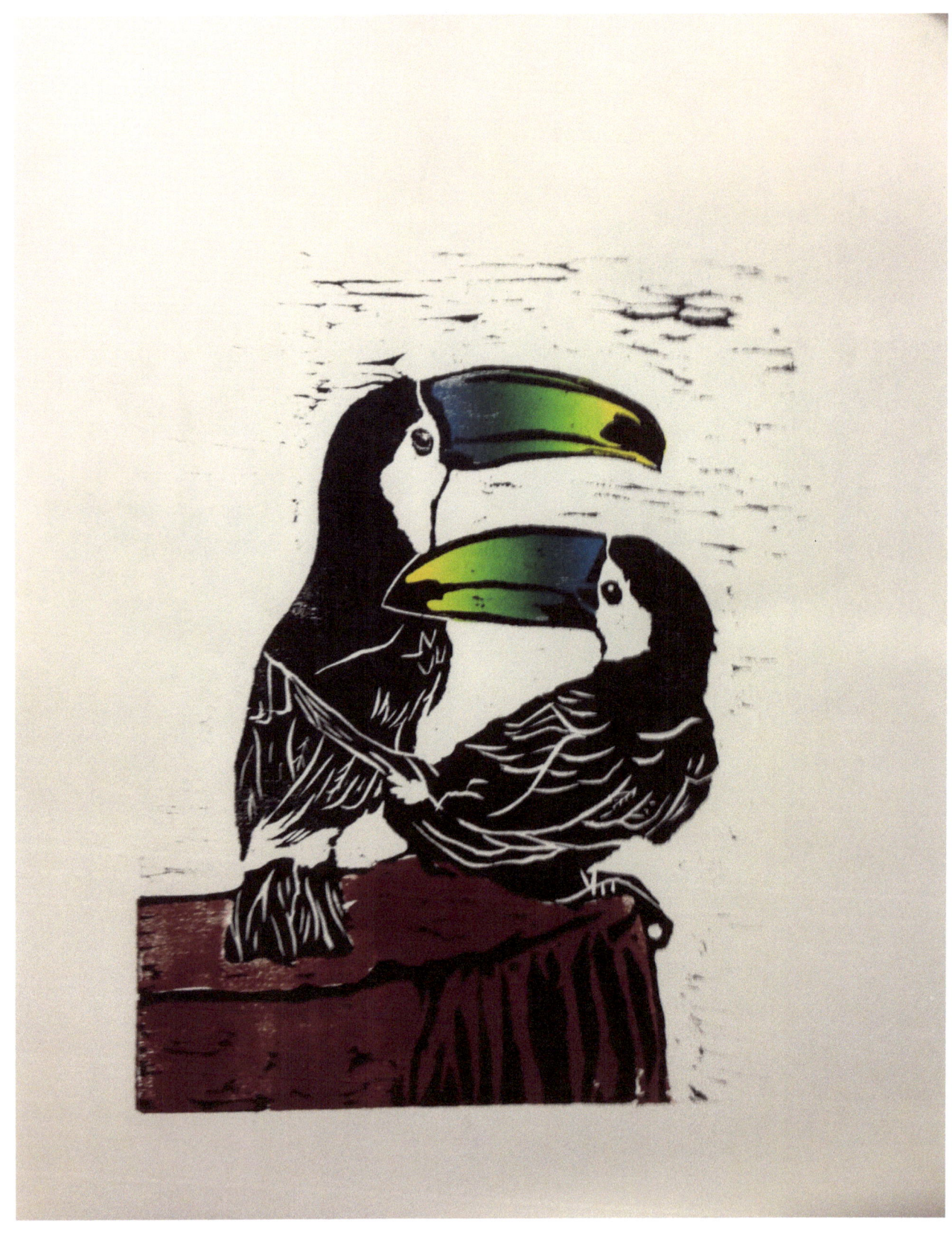

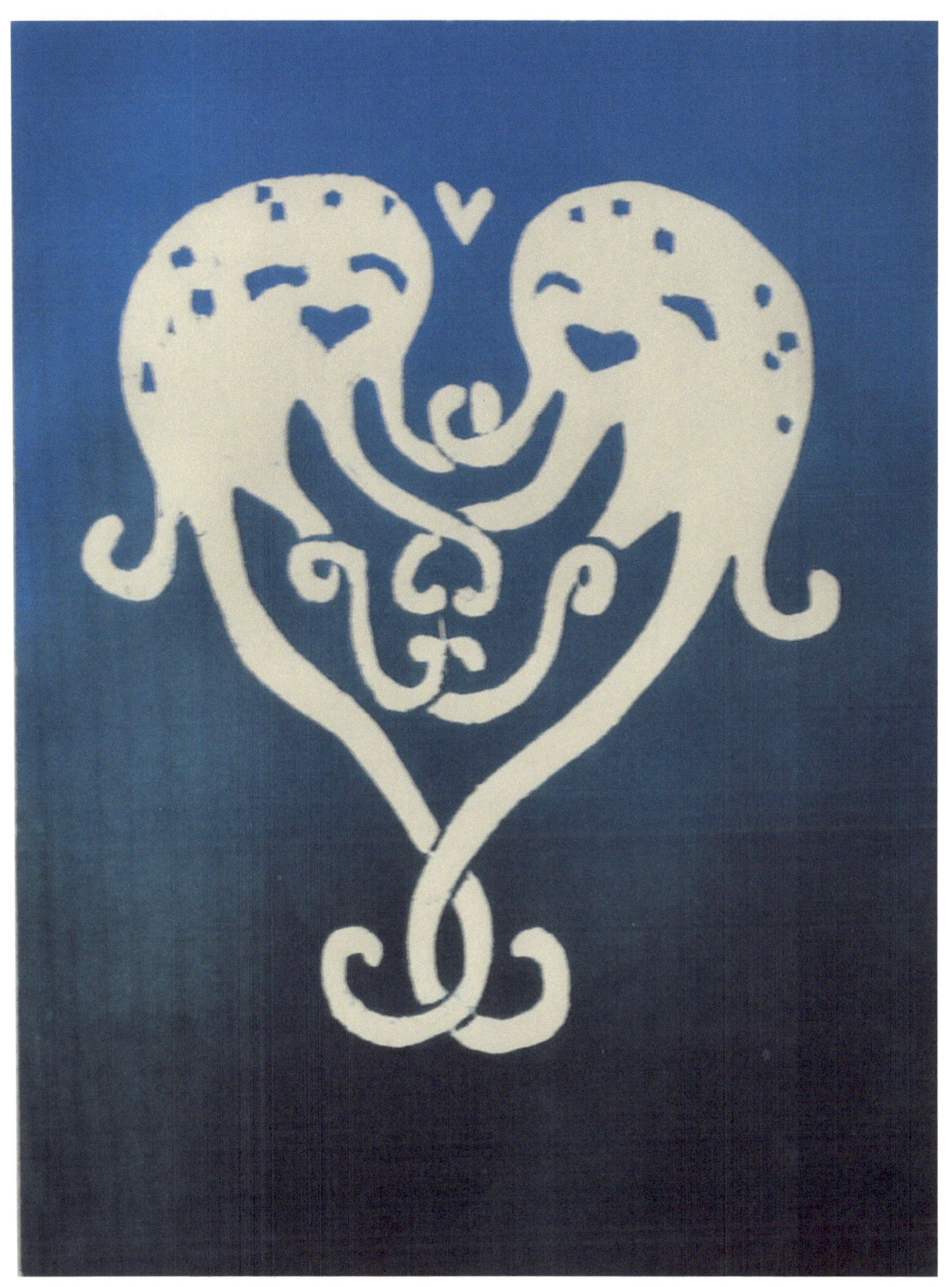

Tangled 2014

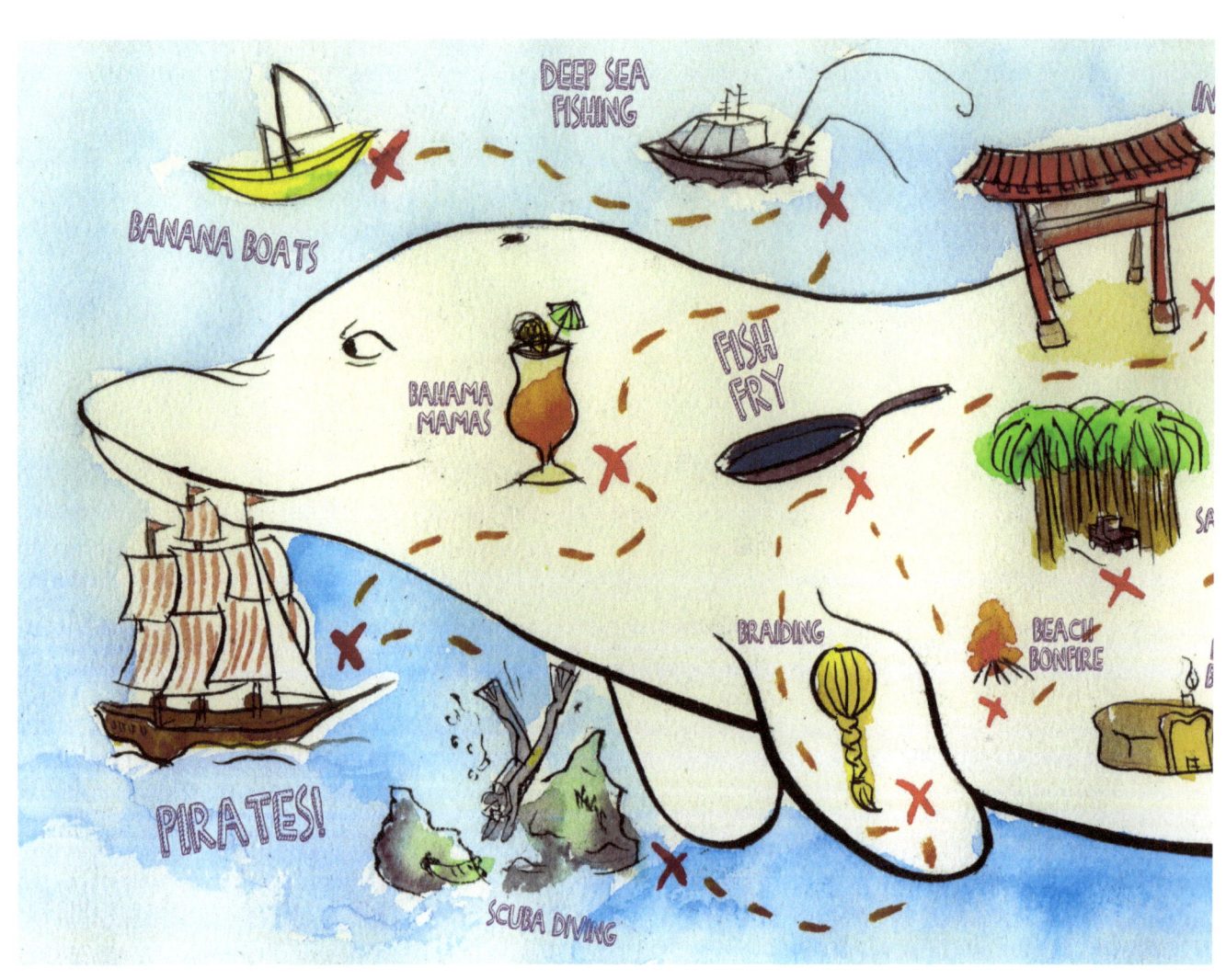

Map of Freeport 2012

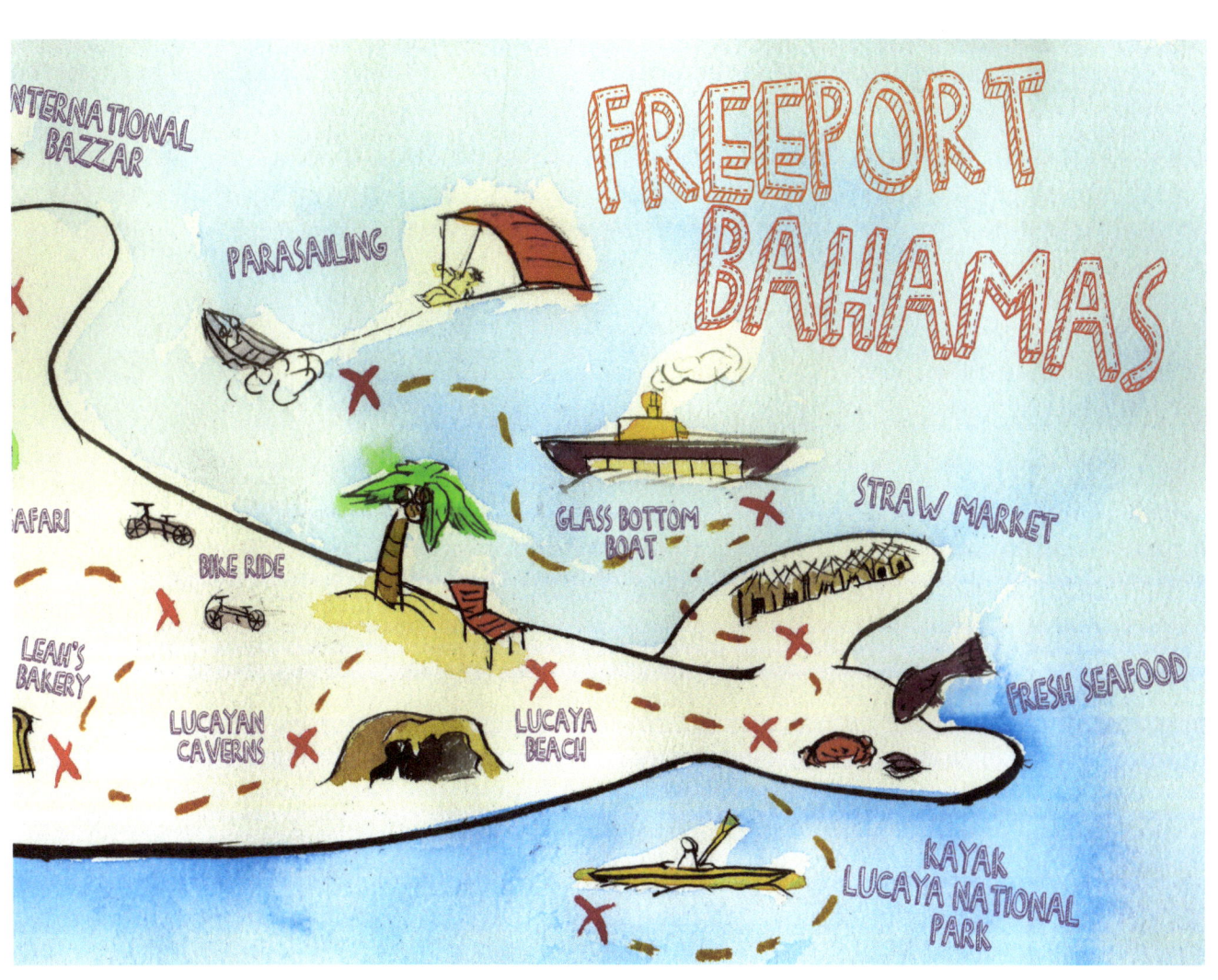

Map of Freeport 2012

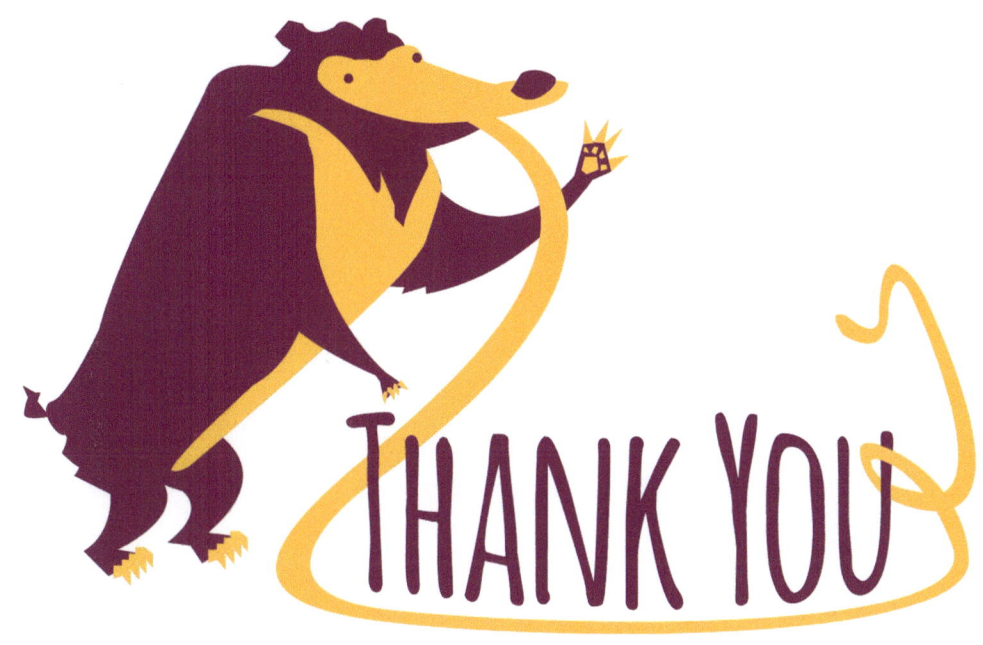

www.ingramcontent.com/pod-product-compliance
Lightning Source LLC
Chambersburg PA
CBHW050910180526
45159CB00007B/2853